Cocktails

Love Food ® is an imprint of Parragon Books Ltd

Parragon
Queen Street House
4 Queen Street
Bath BA1 1HE, UK

Love Food ® and the accompanying heart device is a trade mark of Parragon
Books Ltd

ISBN: 978-1-4075-4328-4

Printed in China

Cover and internal design by Talking Design
Introduction by Linda Doeser

Notes for the reader
This book uses both metric and imperial measurements. Follow the same
units of measurement throughout; do not mix metric with imperial. All spoon
measurements are level, unless otherwise stated: teaspoons are assumed to
be 5 ml and tablespoons are assumed to be 15 ml. Unless otherwise stated,
milk is assumed to be semi-skimmed, eggs and individual vegetables such as
potatoes are medium, and pepper is freshly ground black pepper. Recipes
using raw or very lightly cooked eggs should be avoided by infants, the
elderly, pregnant women, convalescents and anyone suffering from an illness.
The times given are an approximate guide only.

Contents

Introduction 4

Classic Cocktails 8

Contemporary Cocktails 42

Shooters 70

Non-alcoholic Cocktails 98

Index 128

Introduction

Cool and sophisticated, cocktails have always had class. They also have plenty of 21st-century sparkle – they're fun, colourful, inventive, imaginative, taste terrific and are a great way to impress your friends. Cocktails are made for sharing.

It's easy to make and serve cocktails at home, providing you know which should be stirred and which shaken. (The recipes will tell you anyway, but stirred cocktails are clear, while shaken ones are cloudy.) You also need a few pieces of essential equipment and an adequate stock of spirits, mixers, garnishes and glasses. However, unless you're planning to open a cocktail bar, you don't have to rush out and buy everything at once.

Essential Equipment

Jigger The proportions of the ingredients are what makes a good cocktail and, as these are often difficult to work out in millilitres or fluid ounces, quantities in cocktail recipes are given in 'measures'. A jigger is simply a measuring cup for cocktails. The standard size is 25 ml/1 fl oz, but they are available in a variety of sizes and are often double ended.

Cocktail shaker This consists of a container with an inner perforated lid and an outer solid lid. Put cracked ice into the container, immediately pour in the ingredients, secure both lids and shake vigorously for 10–20 seconds, until the outside of the shaker is misted with condensation. Strain the cocktail into a glass through the perforated lid. The aim is to chill the drink during mixing without diluting it with melted ice.

Mixing glass This is a jug for making stirred cocktails. Put cracked ice into the mixing glass, immediately pour in the ingredients, stir vigorously for about 20 seconds, then strain into a glass. As with shaken cocktails, the aim is to chill the drink during mixing without diluting it with melted ice.

Blender Some cocktails are always prepared in a blender and any cocktail that is normally shaken can also be made in a blender.

Bar spoon This long-handled metal spoon is used for stirring cocktails in a mixing glass.

Muddler Rather like a pestle, this is used for lightly mashing ingredients together, as with mint leaves and sugar in a mint julep. You can use a pestle instead.

Bar strainer This is a sort of double strainer that can hold back pieces of ice, fruit fibres and anything else that might spoil the appearance of the cocktail. It is necessary for pouring stirred cocktails and also essential if your cocktail shaker doesn't have a built-in strainer.

Other basics It is worth investing in a good-quality, reliable corkscrew in a style that you find easy to use. You will also need a bottle opener. A sharp knife and chopping board are useful for preparing garnishes and cutting up fruit. An ice bucket and tongs are convenient for keeping ice readily available. Also, make sure that you have plenty of ice in the freezer. A set of standard kitchen measuring spoons and a citrus reamer are also useful.

Glasses You can serve cocktails in virtually any glasses, so if you've already got wine glasses and tall and short tumblers, you're ready to go. Clear uncoloured glass is best for displaying the attractive appearance of many cocktails. For a special occasion, try the following for perfect presentation:

Balloon wine glass Short-stemmed glass with a large bowl holding 300 ml

Champagne flute Tall thin glass holding 125–150 ml

Collins glass Tall narrow glass with straight sides holding 300 ml

Highball glass Tall straight glass holding 225 ml

Margarita glass Stemmed glass with a small bowl topped with a wide saucer shape

Old-fashioned glass Chunky glass holding 225 ml

Shot glass Small glass holding 50 ml

Bartender's Tips

You can stock your bar with the basics over time – it is not necessary to buy everything immediately. A good selection of alcoholic drinks would include US and Irish whiskey, Scotch whisky, brandy, gin, light and dark rum, triple sec, sweet and dry vermouth (martini), vodka and tequila; but select your stock according to your tastes. Standard mixers include club soda, sparkling mineral water, cola, ginger ale, tonic water and fruit juices, such as orange, grapefruit, cranberry and tomato. It is also a good idea to keep a supply of fresh citrus fruits and cocktail cherries for decoration.

Sugar syrup
Many popular cocktails are sweetened with sugar syrup rather than caster sugar which can take a while to dissolve. Pour 6 tablespoons of water into a saucepan, stir in 6 tablespoons of caster sugar and bring to the boil, stirring until the sugar has dissolved. Boil without stirring for 2 minutes, then remove from the heat and leave to cool. Store in a covered container in the refrigerator for up to 2 weeks.

Cracked ice
Put ice cubes between two thick tea towels on a flat surface and hit with a meat mallet or rolling pin until broken into small pieces.

Frosting glasses
The rims of cocktail glasses may be decorated with caster sugar or, occasionally, coarse salt or desiccated coconut. Rub the rim with a wedge of lemon or lime, then dip into a shallow dish of sugar, salt or coconut. Leave to dry.

Chilling glasses
If there's room, chill glasses in the freezer or refrigerator for 2 hours before using. Alternatively, fill the glasses with cracked ice, stir it around briefly, then tip it out before straining in the cocktail.

Layering drinks
Pour in the ingredients in the order listed – syrups (heaviest), liqueurs (middleweight), then spirits (lightest). Pouring them over the back of a spoon, like adding cream to Irish coffee, helps to steady the flow. Let each ingredient settle into a clear layer before adding the next.

Classic Cocktails

Recreate the forbidden excitement of a Chicago speak-easy, the legendary magic of Harry's Bar in Paris, the sophisticated elegance of the American Bar in London's Savoy Hotel or the exotic stylishness of Singapore's Raffles Hotel with this collection of truly cool classics that taste as good today as they did when first invented.

Martini

Serves 1

3 measures gin
1 tsp dry vermouth, or
** to taste**
cracked ice cubes
green cocktail olive,
** to decorate**

For many, this is the ultimate cocktail. It is named after its inventor, Martini de Anna de Toggia, not the famous brand of vermouth!

Shake the gin and vermouth over cracked ice until well frosted.

Strain into a chilled cocktail glass and dress with the cocktail olive.

Manhattan

Serves 1

**dash of Angostura
 bitters**
3 measures rye whiskey
**1 measure sweet
 vermouth**
cracked ice cubes
**cocktail cherry,
 to decorate**

Said to have been invented by Sir Winston Churchill's American mother, Jennie, the Manhattan is one of many cocktails named after places in New York.

Shake the liquids over cracked ice in a mixing glass and mix well.

Strain into a chilled glass and decorate with the cherry.

Margarita

Serves 1

wedge of lime, plus
  extra to decorate
coarse salt
3 measures white
  tequila
1 measure triple sec or
  Cointreau
2 measures lime juice
cracked ice cubes

This cocktail, attributed to Francisco Morales and invented in 1942 in Mexico, is a more civilized version of the original way to drink tequila – lick of salt from the back of your hand, suck of lime juice and a shot of tequila!

Rub the rim of a chilled cocktail glass with the wedge of lime and then dip in a saucer of coarse salt to frost.

Shake the tequila, triple sec and lime juice vigorously over cracked ice until well frosted.

Strain into the prepared glass and decorate with lime.

Daiquiri

Serves 1

2 measures white rum
¾ measure lime juice
½ tsp sugar syrup
cracked ice cubes

Daiquiri is a town in Cuba, where this drink was said to have been invented in the early part of the 20th century. A businessman had run out of imported gin and so had to make do with the local drink – rum – which, at that time, was often of unreliable quality.

Pour the rum, lime juice and sugar syrup over ice and shake vigorously until well frosted.

Strain into a chilled cocktail glass.

Singapore Sling

Serves 1

2 measures gin
1 measure cherry
   brandy
1 measure lemon juice
1 tsp grenadine
cracked ice cubes
soda water
lime peel and cocktail
   cherries, to decorate

In the days of the British Empire, the privileged would gather at their exclusive clubs in the relative cool of the evening to gossip about the day's events. Times may change, but a Singapore Sling is still the ideal thirst-quencher on a hot summer evening.

Shake the gin, cherry brandy, lemon juice and grenadine vigorously over ice until well frosted.

Half fill a chilled glass with cracked ice cubes and strain in the cocktail.

Top off with soda water and decorate with lime peel and cocktail cherries.

Mai Tai

2 measures white rum
2 measures dark rum
1 measure orange
  Curaçao
1 measure lime juice
1 tbsp orgeat
1 tbsp grenadine
cracked ice cubes
slices of pineapple,
  pieces of fruit peel,
  cocktail cherries and
  straws, to decorate

Created in 1944 by restaurateur 'Trader Vic' it was described as 'Mai Tai - Roe Ae' meaning 'out of this world'. It is always flamboyantly dressed.

Shake the white and dark rums, Curaçao, lime juice, orgeat and grenadine vigorously over ice until well frosted.

Strain into a chilled glass and decorate as you wish.

Bellini

Serves 1

**1 measure fresh peach
juice made from
lightly sweetened
liquidized peaches**
caster sugar
**3 measures
Champagne, chilled**

*This delicious concoction was created by Giuseppe
Cipriani at Harry's Bar in Venice, around 1943.*

Dip the rim of a Champagne flute into some peach juice
and then into the sugar to create a sugar-frosted effect.
Set aside to dry. Chill.

Pour the peach juice into the chilled flute and shake
gently.

Top off with Champagne.

Mint Julep

Serves 1

**leaves from 1 fresh
  mint sprig
1 tbsp sugar syrup
crushed ice cubes
3 measures bourbon
  whiskey
fresh mint sprig,
  to decorate**

A julep is simply a mixed drink sweetened with syrup. The Mint Julep was probably first made in the United States, and is the traditional drink of the Kentucky Derby.

Put the mint leaves and sugar syrup into a small chilled glass and mash with a teaspoon or muddler.

Add the crushed ice and shake to mix, before adding the bourbon.

Decorate with the mint sprig.

Whiskey Sour

Serves 1

1 measure lemon or
  lime juice
2 measures blended
  whiskey
1 tsp icing sugar
ice
slice of lemon or lime
  and a maraschino
  cherry, to decorate

Originating in the American South and using some of the best American whiskey, this classic can also be made with vodka, gin or other spirits.

Shake the first three ingredients well over ice and strain into a cocktail glass.

Finish with a slice of lemon or lime and a cherry.

White Lady

Serves 1

2 measures gin
1 measure triple sec
1 measure lemon juice
cracked ice cubes

Simple, elegant, subtle and much more powerful than appearance suggests, this is the perfect cocktail to serve before an alfresco summer dinner.

Shake the gin, triple sec and lemon juice vigorously over ice until well frosted.

Strain into a chilled cocktail glass.

Zombie

Serves 4

2 measures dark rum
2 measures white rum
1 measure golden rum
1 measure triple sec
1 measure lime juice
1 measure orange juice
1 measure pineapple
  juice
1 measure guava juice
1 tbsp grenadine
1 tbsp orgeat
1 tsp Pernod
crushed ice cubes
sprigs of fresh mint and
  wedges of pineapple,
  to decorate

The individual ingredients of this cocktail, including liqueurs and fruit juices, vary considerably from one recipe to another, but all Zombies contain a mixture of white, golden and dark rum in a range of proportions.

Shake all the liquids together over crushed ice until smooth.

Pour, without straining, into a chilled glass.

Decorate with mint and pineapple wedges.

Bloody Mary

Serves I

dash of Worcestershire
  sauce
dash of Tabasco sauce
cracked ice cubes
2 measures vodka
splash of dry sherry
6 measures tomato
  juice
juice of ½ lemon
pinch of celery salt
pinch of cayenne
  pepper
celery stick and slice of
  lemon, to decorate

This classic cocktail was invented in 1921 at the legendary Harry's Bar in Paris. There are numerous versions – some much hotter and spicier. Ingredients may include horseradish sauce in addition to, or instead of, Tabasco sauce.

Dash the Worcestershire sauce and Tabasco sauce over ice in a shaker and add the vodka, splash of dry sherry, tomato juice and lemon juice.

Shake vigorously until frosted.

Strain into a tall chilled glass, add a pinch of celery salt, a pinch of cayenne pepper and decorate with a celery stick and a slice of lemon.

Screwdriver

Serves 1

cracked ice cubes
2 measures vodka
orange juice
slice of orange,
  to decorate

Always use freshly squeezed orange juice to make this refreshing cocktail – it is just not the same with bottled juice. This simple, classic cocktail has given rise to numerous and increasingly elaborate variations.

Fill a chilled glass with cracked ice cubes.

Pour the vodka over the ice and top off with orange juice.

Stir well to mix and dress with a slice of orange.

Long Island Iced Tea

Serves 1

2 measures vodka
1 measure gin
1 measure white tequila
1 measure white rum
½ measure white crème de menthe
2 measures lemon juice
1 tsp sugar syrup
cracked ice cubes
cola
wedge of lime or lemon, to decorate

Dating back to the days of the American Prohibition, when it was drunk out of cups in an attempt to fool the FBI that it was harmless, this cocktail has evolved from the original simple combination of vodka with a dash of cola!

Shake the vodka, gin, tequila, rum, crème de menthe, lemon juice and sugar syrup vigorously over ice until well frosted.

Strain into an ice-filled glass and top off with cola.

Decorate with a lime or lemon wedge.

Moscow Mule

Serves 1

2 measures vodka
1 measure lime juice
cracked ice cubes
ginger beer
slice of lime,
to decorate

This cocktail came into existence through a happy coincidence during the 1930s. An American bar owner had overstocked ginger beer and a representative of a soft drinks company invented the Moscow Mule to help him out.

Shake the vodka and lime juice vigorously over ice until well frosted.

Half fill a chilled glass with cracked ice cubes and strain the cocktail over them.

Top off with ginger beer. Decorate with a slice of lime.

Cranberry Collins

2 measures vodka
¾ measure elderflower
  cordial
3 measures white
  cranberry and apple
  juice or to taste
ice
soda water
slice of lime,
  to decorate

The classic Collins drink is made with gin, but its many variations are made with other spirits so try this one for size...

Shake the first three ingredients over ice until well frosted.

Strain into a Collins glass with more ice and top off with soda to taste.

Decorate with a slice of lime.

Contemporary Cocktails

As each generation discovers the delights of cocktails, the repertoire increases. New ingredients are incorporated, more daring mixtures are combined and even the names reflect a new culture and a different sense of humour. What remains the same is the superb blending of wonderful flavours in a single glass.

Cosmopolitan

Serves 1

2 measures vodka
1 measure triple sec
1 measure fresh lime juice
1 measure cranberry juice
ice
strip of orange zest, to decorate

Inviting and refreshing, the Cosmopolitan is the beverage of choice for the 'Sex and the City' girls and is a must at any fashionable party.

Shake all the liquid ingredients over ice until well frosted.

Strain into a chilled cocktail glass.

Decorate with a strip of orange zest.

Sex on the Beach

Serves 1

1 measure peach
  schnapps
1 measure vodka
2 measures fresh
  orange juice
3 measures cranberry
  and peach juice
ice and crushed ice
dash of lemon juice
piece of orange zest,
  to decorate

Holiday drinks are often long and fruity and this
refreshing cocktail is reminiscent of happy days in
the sun.

Shake the peach schnapps, vodka, orange juice, and
cranberry and peach juice over ice until well frosted.

Strain into a glass filled with crushed iced and squeeze
over the lemon juice.

Decorate with orange zest.

Piña Colada

Serves 1

2 measures white rum
1 measure dark rum
3 measures pineapple juice
2 measures coconut cream
4–6 crushed ice cubes
wedges of pineapple, to decorate

One of the younger generation of classics, this became popular during the cocktail revival of the 1980s and has remained so ever since.

Shake the white rum, dark rum, pineapple juice and coconut cream over the crushed ice until combined.

Pour, without straining, into a tall, chilled glass and decorate with pineapple wedges.

Sangria

juice of 1 orange
juice of 1 lemon
2 tbsp caster sugar
ice cubes
1 orange, thinly sliced
1 lemon, thinly sliced
1 bottle red wine,
  chilled
lemonade

A perfect long cold drink for a crowd of friends at a summer barbecue!

Shake the orange and lemon juice with the sugar and transfer to a large bowl or jug.

When the sugar has dissolved, add a few ice cubes, the sliced fruit and wine.

Marinate for 1 hour if possible, and then add lemonade to taste and more ice.

Club Mojito

Serves 1

1 tsp sugar syrup
a few mint leaves
juice of ½ lime
ice
2 measures dark rum
soda water
dash of Angostura
  bitters
mint leaves,
  to decorate

Dark rum is rich in flavour and redolent of sunshine holiday memories.

Put the syrup, mint leaves and lime juice into a glass and muddle the mint leaves.

Add the ice and rum and shake well, pour into a glass and top off with soda water to taste.

Finish with a dash of Angostura bitters and decorate with mint leaves.

Harvey Wallbanger

Serves 1

ice cubes
3 measures vodka
8 measures orange juice
2 tsp Galliano
cocktail cherry and slice of orange, to decorate

This well-known contemporary classic cocktail is a great party drink – mix it strong at first, then weaker as the evening goes by – or without alcohol for drivers and no one would know…!

Half fill a glass with ice, pour the vodka and orange juice over the ice cubes, and float Galliano on top.

Decorate with a cherry and slice of orange.

For a warming variant, mix a splash of ginger wine with the vodka and orange juice.

Seabreeze

Serves 1

1½ measures vodka
½ measure cranberry juice
ice
pink grapefruit juice

Pink grapefruit juice is much sweeter and subtler than its paler cousin, so it is ideal to mix in cocktails where you want just a slight sharpness.

Shake the vodka and cranberry juice over ice until frosted.

Pour into a chilled tumbler or long glass and top off with pink grapefruit juice to taste.

Serve with a straw.

Blue Lagoon

Serves 1

1 measure blue Curaçao
1 measure vodka
dash of fresh lemon juice
lemonade

Let your imagination carry you away while you sink into this luxuriously blue cocktail. It has a refreshing lemon zing and sparkle too.

Pour the blue Curaçao into a highball or cocktail glass, followed by the vodka.

Add the lemon juice and top off with lemonade to taste.

Fuzzy Navel

Serves 1

2 measures vodka
1 measure peach schnapps
250 ml/8 fl oz orange juice
cracked ice cubes
Cape gooseberry, to decorate

This is another one of those cocktails with a name that plays on the ingredients - fuzzy to remind you that it contains peach schnapps and navel because it is mixed with orange juice.

Shake the vodka, peach schnapps and orange juice vigorously over cracked ice until well frosted.

Strain into a chilled cocktail glass and decorate with a Cape gooseberry.

Woo-Woo

Serves 1

cracked ice cubes
2 measures vodka
2 measures peach
  schnapps
4 measures cranberry
  juice
Cape gooseberry,
  to decorate

Be sure to woo your friends with this refreshing and simple drink. It's also great for parties.

Half fill a chilled cocktail glass with cracked ice.

Pour the vodka, peach schnapps and cranberry juice over the ice.

Stir well to mix and decorate with a Cape gooseberry.

Black Russian

Serves 1

2 measures vodka
1 measure coffee
** liqueur**
4–6 cracked ice cubes

History records only White and Red Russians. The omission of the Black Russian is a sad oversight. For a coffee liqueur, you can use either Tia Maria or Kahlúa, depending on your personal taste – the latter is sweeter.

Pour the vodka and coffee liqueur over cracked ice cubes in a small chilled glass.

Stir to mix.

Mudslide

Serves I

1½ measures Kahlúa
**1½ measures Baileys
 Irish Cream**
1½ measures vodka
cracked ice cubes

Despite its ominous-sounding name, this is a richly flavoured creamy concoction that is delicious whatever the weather.

Shake the Kahlúa, Baileys Irish Cream and vodka vigorously over ice until well frosted.

Strain into a chilled glass.

Chocolate Martini

Serves 1

2 measures vodka
¼ measure crème de cacao
2 dashes of orange flower water
cocoa powder, to decorate

For many, this is the ultimate cocktail. It is named after its inventor, Martini de Anna de Toggia.

Shake the vodka, crème de cacao and orange flower water over ice until really well frosted.

Strain into a cocktail glass rimmed with cocoa powder.

Shooters

Shots, shooters and slammers are little drinks that pack a punch. Always imaginative, often colourful, frequently surprising and usually with outrageous names, these cocktails are based on an astonishing range of liqueurs and spirits and invariably include a good measure of fun.

Tequila Shot

Serves 1

**1 measure white tequila, chilled
1 measure lemon juice
sparkling wine, chilled**

Slammers are a type of shooter. The idea is that you pour the ingredients directly into the glass, without stirring. Cover the glass with one hand to prevent spillage, slam it onto a table to mix and drink the cocktail down in one! Do ensure you use a strong glass!

Put the tequila and lemon juice into a chilled glass.

Top up with sparkling wine.

Cover the glass with your hand and slam.

Alabama Slammer

Serves 1

1 measure Southern Comfort
1 measure Amaretto
½ measure sloe gin
cracked ice cubes
½ tsp lemon juice

Small, but perfectly proportioned – this is a shooter with a real kick!

Pour the Southern Comfort, Amaretto and sloe gin over cracked ice in a mixing glass and stir.

Strain into a shot glass and add the lemon juice.

Cover and slam.

Maidenly Mimosa

Serves 2

175 ml/6 fl oz freshly
squeezed orange juice
175 ml/6 fl oz sparkling
white grape juice

This simple but chic drink is the perfect non-alcoholic alternative to the classic champagne cocktail. Use freshly squeezed orange juice for maximum flavour.

Divide the orange juice between 2 chilled wine glasses or champagne flutes.

Top off with the grape juice and serve.

Soft Sangria

Makes 2 litres/3½ pints

1.5 litres/2¾ pints red
 grape juice
300 ml/10 fl oz orange
 juice
75 ml/2½ fl oz
 cranberry juice
50 ml/2 fl oz lemon
 juice
50 ml/2 fl oz lime juice
100 ml/3½ fl oz sugar
 syrup
ice cubes

To decorate
slices of lemon
slices of orange
slices of lime

This is an alternative to the well-known Spanish wine cup whose potency has caught out many an unwary tourist! This alcohol-free version poses no risk of intoxication.

Put the grape juice, orange juice, cranberry juice, lemon juice, lime juice and sugar syrup into a chilled punch bowl and stir well.

Add the ice and decorate with the slices of lemon, orange and lime.

Cherry Kiss

Serves 2

**8 ice cubes, crushed
2 tbsp cherry syrup
500 ml/18 fl oz
 sparkling water
fresh cherries on long
 swizzle sticks,
 to decorate**

A great party drink for those avoiding alcohol, this cherry drink tastes as good as it looks.

Divide the crushed ice between two glasses and pour over the cherry syrup.

Top off each glass with sparkling water. Decorate with the cherries on long swizzle sticks and serve.

Mint & Cucumber Refresher

Serves 1

a few sprigs mint
1 tsp caster sugar
juice of 1 lime
2 cm/¾ inch piece
 cucumber, thinly
 sliced
sparkling mineral
 water, chilled
ice cubes

This is great to serve at a summer party. The cucumber inside the glass will be a real talking point!

Chop a few of the mint leaves and mix with the sugar.

Rub a little lime juice round the rim of a pretty glass and dip in the minted sugar. Leave to dry.

Mix the remaining lime juice, cucumber, and the remaining mint leaves – some chopped and some whole – in a jug and chill.

To serve, pour the lime and cucumber mixture into the prepared glass and top up with chilled sparkling water and ice cubes to taste.

Pomegranate Passion

Serves 2

2 ripe pomegranates
I passion fruit
I tbsp clear honey
crushed ice

This is a lovely late summer drink made with the new season's pomegranates, which start to appear in the shops in August.

Cut the pomegranates in half and extract the juice with an old-fashioned lemon squeezer.

Halve the passion fruit and sieve the pulp into a small bowl. Mix in the pomegranate juice and honey.

Pour over the crushed ice, add a straw and serve.

Cool Cranberries

Serves 4

350 g/12 oz cranberries, thawed if frozen
425 ml/15 fl oz cranberry juice, chilled
300 ml/10 fl oz natural yogurt
2–3 tbsp clear honey

Cranberries can make a wonderfully colourful and tasty drink. This is a great way to encourage your children to eat more fruit.

Place the berries and juice in a blender and process until smooth. Add the yogurt and the honey and process again until combined. Taste and add more honey if necessary.

Pour into chilled glasses and serve.

Summer Fruit Slush

Serves 2

4 tbsp orange juice
1 tbsp lime juice
100 ml/3½ fl oz
  sparkling mineral
  water
350 g/12 oz frozen
  summer fruits
  (such as blueberries,
  raspberries,
  blackberries
  and strawberries)
4 ice cubes

This medley of summer berries makes an inspired drink. Packed-full of vitamins, it is as healthy as it is refreshing.

Pour the orange juice, lime juice and sparkling water into a food processor and process gently until combined.

Add the summer fruits and ice cubes and process until a slushy consistency has been reached.

Pour the mixture into glasses and serve

Banana & Apple Booster

Serves 2

250 ml/9 fl oz apple juice
½ tsp powdered cinnamon
2 tsp grated fresh ginger
2 bananas, sliced and frozen
chunks of fresh apple on cocktail sticks, to decorate

This invigorating drink is spiked with warming ginger and cinnamon for an added kick without the alcohol.

Pour the apple juice into a food processor. Add the cinnamon and ginger and process gently until combined.

Add the bananas and process until smooth. Pour the mixture into glasses and decorate with chunks of fresh apple on cocktail sticks. Serve immediately.

Pineapple Tango

Serves 2

125 ml/4 fl oz
   pineapple juice
juice of 1 lemon
100 ml/3½ fl oz water
3 tbsp brown sugar
175 ml/6 fl oz natural
   yogurt
1 peach, cut into
   chunks and frozen
100 g/3½ oz frozen
   pineapple chunks
wedges of pineapple,
   to decorate

This cooling thirst quencher is an alcohol-free alternative to the classic Piña Colada. It is an ideal refresher on long, hot summer days.

Pour the pineapple juice, lemon juice and water into a food processor. Add the sugar and yogurt and process until blended.

Add the peach and pineapple chunks and process until smooth.

Pour the mixture into glasses and decorate the rims with wedges of fresh pineapple.

Serve immediately.

Coffee Banana Cooler

Serves 2

300 ml/10 fl oz milk
4 tbsp instant coffee powder
150 g/5½ oz vanilla ice cream
2 bananas, sliced and frozen

This creamy mikshake combines the ever-popular flavours of banana and coffee with rich vanilla ice cream for the ultimate chilled drink.

Pour the milk into a food processor, add the coffee powder and process gently until combined. Add half of the vanilla ice cream and process gently, then add the remaining ice cream and process until well combined.

When the mixture is thoroughly blended, add the bananas and process until smooth.

Pour the mixture into glasses and serve.

Alabama Slammer 74
Amaretto: Alabama Slammer 74
apple juice
    Banana & Apple Booster 123
    Cranberry Collins 40
apricot brandy: Fifth Avenue 89

B-52 90
Baileys Irish Cream
    B-52 90
    Brain Hemorrhage 83
    Mudslide 67
Banana & Apple Booster 123
bananas
    Banana & Apple Booster 123
    Coffee Banana Cooler 126
Bellini 22
Black Russian 64
Bloody Mary 33
Blue Lagoon 58
Brain Haemorrhage 83

Champagne: Bellini 22
Chartreuse: Nuclear Fallout 80
cherry brandy: Singapore Sling 18
Cherry Kiss 112
cherry syrup: Cherry Kiss 112
Chocolate Martini 68
Club Mojito 52
Coffee Banana Cooler 126
coffee liqueur: Black Russian 64
coffee powder: Coffee Banana
    Cooler 126
Cointreau
    Margarita 15
    Margarita Jelly Shot 96
    Nuclear Fallout 80
Cool Cranberries 118
Cosmopolitan 44
Cowboy 77
Cranberry Collins 40
cranberry juice
    Cool Cranberries 118
    Cosmopolitan 44
    Cranberry Collins 40
    Peach Floyd 78
    Seabreeze 56
    Sex on the Beach 46
    Soft Sangria 111
    Woo-Woo 62
cream
    Cowboy 77
    Fifth Avenue 89
crème de cacao
    B-52 90
    Chocolate Martini 68
    Fifth Avenue 89
    Peppermint Patty 92
crème de menthe
    Long Island Iced Tea 36
    Peppermint Patty 92
Curaçao
    Blue Lagoon 58

Mai Tai 21
Nuclear Fallout 80

Daiquiri 16
Drambuie: Toffee Split 86

Faux Kir 106
Fifth Avenue 89
Fuzzy Navel 61

Galliano: Harvey Wallbanger 55
gin
    Long Island Iced Tea 36
    Martini 10
    Singapore Sling 18
    White Lady 28
ginger ale
    Juicy Julep 102
    Shirley Temple 105
ginger beer: Moscow Mule 39
Grand Marnier: B-52 90
grape juice
    Faux Kir 106
    Maidenly Mimosa 108
    Soft Sangria 111
grapefruit juice: Seabreeze 56
grenadine
    Brain Hemorrhage 83
    Island Cooler 100
    Mai Tai 21
    Shirley Temple 105
    Singapore Sling 18
    Zombie 30

Harvey Wallbanger 55
honey
    Cool Cranberries 118
    Pomegranate Passion 117

ice cream: Coffee Banana Cooler 126
Island Cooler 100

jelly
    Margarita Jelly Shot 96
    Whiskey Sour Jelly Shot 95
Juicy Julep 102

Kahlúa: Mudslide 67

lemon juice
    Island Cooler 100
    Long Island Iced Tea 36
    Pineapple Tango 124
    Sangria 50
    Shirley Temple 105
    Singapore Sling 18
    Soft Sangria 111
    Whiskey Sour 27
    White Lady 28
lemonade: Blue Lagoon 58
lime juice
    Club Mojito 52
    Cosmopolitan 44
    Daiquiri 16
    Juicy Julep 102
    Mai Tai 21
    Margarita 15
    Mint & Cucumber Refresher 114
    Moscow Mule 39
    Soft Sangria 111
    Summer Fruit Slush 120

Whiskey Sour 27
Zombie 30
Long Island Iced Tea 36

Mai Tai 21
Maidenly Mimosa 108
Manhattan 12
maraschino liqueur: Nuclear
    Fallout 80
Margarita 15
Margarita Jelly Shot 96
Martini 10
Mint & Cucumber Refresher 114
Mint Julep 24
Moscow Mule 39
Mudslide 67

Nuclear Fallout 80

orange juice
    Fuzzy Navel 61
    Harvey Wallbanger 55
    Island Cooler 100
    Juicy Julep 102
    Maidenly Mimosa 108
    Sangria 50
    Screwdriver 34
    Sex on the Beach 46
    Soft Sangria 111
    Summer Fruit Slush 120
    Zombie 30

passion fruit: Pomegranate
    Passion 117
pawpaw juice: Island Cooler 100
Peach Floyd 78
peach juice
    Bellini 22
    Peach Floyd 78
    Sex on the Beach 46
Peppermint Patty 92
Pernod: Zombie 30
Piña Colada 49
pineapple juice
    Island Cooler 100
    Juicy Julep 102
    Piña Colada 49
    Pineapple Tango 124
    Zombie 30
Pineapple Tango 124
pomegranate juice: Pomegranate
    Passion 117

raspberry syrup
    Faux Kir 106
    Juicy Julep 102
    Nuclear Fallout 80
red wine: Sangria 50
rum
    Club Mojito 52
    Daiquiri 16
    Long Island Iced Tea 36
    Mai Tai 21
    Piña Colada 49
    Zombie 30

Sambuca: Tornado 84
Sangria 50
schnapps
    Brain Hemorrhage 83
    Fuzzy Navel 61
    Peach Floyd 78

Sex on the Beach 46
Tornado 84
Woo-Woo 62
Screwdriver 34
Seabreeze 56
Sex on the Beach 46
sherry: Bloody Mary 33
Shirley Temple 105
Singapore Sling 18
sloe gin: Alabama Slammer 74
Soft Sangria 111
Southern Comfort: Alabama
    Slammer 74
sparkling wine: Tequila Shot 72
Summer Fruit Slush 120

tequila
    Long Island Iced Tea 36
    Margarita 15
    Margarita Jelly Shot 96
    Tequila Shot 72
Tequila Shot 72
toffee liqueur: Toffee Split 86
Toffee Split 86
tomato juice: Bloody Mary 33
Tornado 84
triple sec
    Cosmopolitan 44
    Margarita 15
    White Lady 28
    Zombie 30

vermouth
    Manhattan 12
    Martini 10
vodka
    Black Russian 64
    Bloody Mary 33
    Blue Lagoon 58
    Chocolate Martini 68
    Cosmopolitan 44
    Cranberry Collins 40
    Fuzzy Navel 61
    Harvey Wallbanger 55
    Long Island Iced Tea 36
    Moscow Mule 39
    Mudslide 67
    Peach Floyd 78
    Screwdriver 34
    Seabreeze 56
    Sex on the Beach 46
    Woo-Woo 62

Whiskey Sour 27
Whiskey Sour Jelly Shot 95
whiskey
    Cowboy 77
    Manhattan 12
    Mint Julep 24
    Whiskey Sour 27
    Whiskey Sour Jelly Shot 95
White Lady 28
Woo-Woo 62

yogurt
    Cool Cranberries 118
    Pineapple Tango 124

Zombie 30